A TREASURY
of
Playtime
Poems

Compiled by
Robin G. J. Crouch

Ideals Children's Books • Nashville, Tennessee

Art titles and authors in order of appearance:

Romping	William Marshall Brown
The Flute	George Smith
Portrait of the Artist's Daughter	Arthur Rackham
Cheap Entertainment	Joseph Clark
Dressing Up	Hamilton Hamilton
Swinging Along	Anonymous
Daisy Chains	Thomas Bromley Blacklock
Learning to Swim	Arthur John Elsley
The Fishing Expedition	Johan Mari Henri Ten Kate
Good Afternoon	Ernest Walbourn
Romping	William Marshall Brown
On the Beach	William Lionel Wyllie
Burning Leaves	Henry LeJeune
Playing at School	Charles James Lewis
Twenty Miles an Hour	William Luson Thomas
Blind Man's Bluff	Anonymous
Spring Flowers	Myles Birket Foster
The First of May	Myles Birket Foster

Published by Ideals Publishing Corporation
Nashville, Tennessee 37214

Designed by Susan Harrison

The illustrations in this book are
full-color reproductions of oil paintings, courtesy of
Art Licensing International, Inc., agents for
Fine Art Photographs, London.

Printed and bound in the United States of America

Library of Congress Cataloging-in-Publication Data

A treasury of playtime poems.

Includes index.
Summary: An illustrated collection of classic children's
poems by writers including Robert Louis Stevenson,
William Blake, and Kenneth Grahame.
1. Children's poetry, English. 2. Children's poetry,
American. [1. English poetry—Collections. 2. American
poetry—Collections] I. Crouch, Robin G. J.
PR1175.3.T73   1990   821.008'09282   90-4580
ISBN 0-8249-8485-4

TABLE OF CONTENTS

COMPANIONS AT PLAY:

FAMILY FRIENDS

When you and I grow up, Polly,
*   I mean that you and me,*
Shall go sailing in a big ship
*   Right over all the sea.*
We'll wait till we are older,
*   For if we went today,*
You know that we might lose ourselves,
*   And never find the way.*

Kate Greenaway

REEDS OF INNOCENCE

William Blake

Piping down the valleys wild,
　　Piping songs of pleasant glee,
On a cloud I saw a child,
　　And he laughing said to me:

"Pipe a song about a Lamb!"
　　So I piped with merry cheer.
"Piper, pipe that song again."
　　So I piped: He wept to hear.

"Drop thy pipe, thy happy pipe;
　　Sing thy songs of happy cheer!"
So I sang the same again,
　　While he wept with joy to hear.

"Piper, sit thee down and write
　　In a book that all may read."
So he vanished from my sight,
　　And I plucked a hollow reed,

And I made a rural pen,
　　And I stain'd the water clear,
And I wrote my happy songs
　　Every child may joy to hear.

I REMEMBER, I REMEMBER

Thomas Hood

I remember, I remember
The house where I was born,
The little window where the sun
Came peeping in at morn;

I remember, I remember
The roses, red and white,
The violets, and the lily-cups—
Those flowers made of light!

I remember, I remember
Where I used to swing,
And thought the air must rush as fresh
To swallows on the wing.

I remember, I remember
The fir trees dark and high;
I used to think their slender tops
Were close against the sky.

WISHING

William Allingham

I wish I were a robin,
A robin or a little wren, everywhere to go;
    Through forest, field, or garden,
    And ask no leave or pardon,
Till Winter comes with icy thumbs
To ruffle up our wing!

    Where should I fly to,
Where to go to sleep in the dark wood or dell?
    Before a day was over,
    Home comes the rover,
For Mother's kiss—sweeter this
Than any other thing!

GOOD NIGHT AND GOOD MORNING

Richard Monckton Milnes

A fair girl sat under a tree
   Sewing as long as her eyes could see;
Then smoothed her work and folded it right,
   And said, "Dear work, good night, good night!"

And while on her pillow she softly lay,
   She knew nothing more till again it was day,
And all good things said to the beautiful sun,
   "Good morning, good morning, our work is begun."

I WILL MAKE YOU BROOCHES

Robert Louis Stevenson

I will make you brooches
   And toys for your delight
Of birdsong at morning
   And starshine at night.
I will make a palace
   Fit for you and me,
Of green days in forests
   And blue days at sea.

MOTHER AND I

Eugene Field

O Mother-my-love, if you'll give me your hand,
 And go where I ask you to wander,
I will lead you away to this beautiful land—
 The dreamland that's waiting out yonder.
We'll walk in a sweet posy garden out there,
 Where moonlight and starlight are streaming,
And the flowers and the birds are filling the air
 With the fragrance and music of dreaming.

There'll be no little tired-out boy to undress,
 No questions or cares to perplex you;
There'll be no little bruises or bumps to caress,
 Nor patching of socks to vex you.
For I'll rock you away on a silver-dew stream,
 And sing you asleep when you're weary,
And no one shall know of our beautiful dream
 But you and your own little dearie.

LOVE BETWEEN BROTHERS AND SISTERS
Isaac Watts

Whatever brawls disturb the street,
    There should be peace at home.
Where sisters dwell and brothers meet,
    Quarrels should never come.

Birds in their little nests agree;
    And 'tis a shameful sight,
When children of one family
    Fall out and chide and fight.

WE THANK THEE
Anonymous

For mother-love and father-care,
For brothers strong and sisters fair,
For love at home and here each day,
For guidance lest we go astray,
    Father in Heaven, we thank thee.

I LIKE LITTLE PUSSY

Jane Taylor

I like little Pussy,
   Her coat is so warm;
And if I don't hurt her
   She'll do me no harm.
So I'll not pull her tail,
   Nor drive her away,
But Pussy and I
   Very gently will play;
She shall sit by my side,
   And I'll give her some food;
And she'll love me because
   I am gentle and good.

I'll pat little Pussy,
   And then she will purr,
And thus show her thanks
   For my kindness to her;
I'll not pinch her ears,
   Nor tread on her paw,
Lest I should provoke her
   To use her sharp claw;
I never will vex her,
   Nor make her displeased,
For Pussy can't bear
   To be worried or teased.

THE LAND OF DREAMS

William Blake

"Awake, awake, my little boy!
Thou wast thy mother's only joy;
Why dost thou weep in thy gentle sleep?
O wake! Thy father doth thee keep.

O what is the land of dreams?
What are its mountains and what are its streams?"
"O father, I saw my mother there,
Among the lilies by waters fair."

"Dear child! I also by pleasant streams
Have wandered all night in the land of dreams,
But, though calm and warm the waters wide,
I could not get to the other side."

"Father, O Father! What do we here,
In this land of unbelief and fear?
The land of dreams is better far,
Above the light of the morning star."

CHILDHOOD FRIENDS

I have had playmates,
I have had companions,
In my days of childhood,
In my joyful school days.

Charles Lamb

DELIGHT IN DISORDER
Robert Herrick

A sweet disorder in the dress
Kindles in clothes a wantonness:
A lawn about the shoulders thrown
Into a fine distraction;

An erring lace, which here and there
Enthralls the crimson stomacher;
A cuff neglectful, and thereby
Ribbons to flow confusedly;

A winning wave, deserving note
In the tempestuous petticoat;
A careless shoestring, in whose tie
I see a wild civility,
Do more bewitch me, than when art
Is too precise in every part.

THE ARROW AND THE SONG

Henry Wadsworth Longfellow

I shot an arrow into the air,
It fell to earth, I knew not where;
For, so swiftly it flew, the sight
Could not follow it in its flight.

I breathed a song into the air,
It fell to earth, I knew not where;
For who has sight so keen and strong
That it can follow the flight of a song?

Long, long afterward, in an oak,
I found the arrow still unbroke;
And the song, from beginning to end,
I found again in the heart of a friend.

TO A CHILD

William Wordsworth

Small service is true service while it lasts:
Of humblest friends, bright creature! Scorn not one:
The daisy, by the shadow it casts,
Protects the lingering dewdrop from the sun.

A LITTLE BOY'S POCKET

Anonymous

Do you know what's in my pottet?
  Such a lot of treasures in it!
Listen now while I bedin it:
  Such a lot of sings it holds,
And everysin dats in my pottet,
  And when, and where, and how I dot it.
First of all, here's in my pottet
A beauty shell, I pit'd it up:
  And here's the handle of a tup
That somebody has broked at tea;
  The shell's a hole in it, you see:
Nobody knows dat I dot it,
  I teep it safe here in my pottet.
And here's my pennies, one, two, free,
  That Aunty Mary gave to me.
Here's my lead, and here's my string;
  I once had an iron ring.
But through a hole it lost one day,
  And this is what I always say—
A hole's the worst sing in a pottet,
  Be sure and mend it when you've dot it.

25

THE SWING

Robert Louis Stevenson

How do you like to go up in a swing,
    Up in the air so blue?
Oh, I think it the pleasantest thing
    Ever a child can do!

Up in the air and over the wall,
    Till I can see so wide,
Rivers and trees and cattle and all
    Over the countryside—

Till I look down on the garden green;
    Down on the roof so brown—
Up in the air I go flying again,
    Up in the air and down!

A GIRL'S SONG

Thomas Moore

There's a bower of roses by Bendemeer's stream,
And the nightingale sings 'round it all the day long;
In the time of my childhood 'twas like a sweet dream
To sit in the roses and hear the bird's song.

That bower and its music I never forget,
But oft when alone in the bloom of the year,
I think—is the nightingale singing there yet?
Are the roses still bright by the calm Bendemeer?

No, the roses soon withered that hung o'er the wave,
But some blossoms were gathered while freshly they
    shone,
And a dew was distilled from their flowers that gave
All the fragrance of summer when summer was gone.

Thus memory draws from delight, ere it dies,
An essence that breathes of it many a year;
Thus bright to my soul, as 'twas then to my eyes,
Is that bower on the banks of the calm Bendemeer!

A GOOD PLAY

Robert Louis Stevenson

We built a ship upon the stairs,
All made of back-bedroom chairs,
And filled it full of sofa pillows
To go a-sailing on the billows.

We took a saw and several nails,
And water in the nursery pails;
And Tom said, "Let us also take
An apple and a slice of cake,"
Which was enough for Tom and me
To go a-sailing on till tea.

We sailed along for days and days,
And had the very best of plays;
But Tom fell out and hurt his knee,
So there was no one left but me.

CHILDHOOD

Anonymous

When birdsongs and hens fill
    the barnyard air,
And from byre there comes
    the lowing,
When mist on the hills is
    rising fair,
All the little feet are going.

The game of tag and the bare
    pony ride,
The boat on the water
    gleaming,
The peat fire of evening and
    tale beside,
Fill daytime till bedtime
    dreaming.

O God bless the girl and God
    bless the boy,
No ragwort-whip may they
    merit,
And as they grow be they
    filled with thy joy,
Thy kingdom may they
    inherit.

THE BAREFOOT BOY
John Greenleaf Whittier

Blessings on thee, little man,
Barefoot boy, with cheek of tan!
With thy turned-up pantaloons,
And thy merry whistled tunes;
With thy red lips, redder still
Kissed by strawberries on the hill;
With the sunshine on thy face,
Through thy torn brim's jaunty grace;
From my heart I give thee joy—
I was once a barefoot boy!

THE LITTLE GENTLEMAN
Anonymous

Take your meals, my little man,
Always be a gentleman;
Wash your face and hands with care,
Change your shoes and brush your hair;

Do not rudely point or touch:
Do not eat or drink too much.
Seek in all things that you can
To be a little gentleman.

ANIMAL FRIENDS

Of all beasts he learned the language,
Learned their names and all their secrets,
How the beavers built their lodges,
Where the squirrels hid their acorns,
How the reindeer ran so swiftly,
Why the rabbit was so timid,
Talked with them whene'er he met them,
Called them "Hiawatha's brothers."

Henry Wadsworth Longfellow

DUCK'S DITTY

Kenneth Grahame

All along the backwater,
Through the rushes tall,
Ducks are a-dabbling,
Up tails all!

Duck's tails, drake's tales,
Yellow feet a-quiver,
Yellow bills all out of sight
Busy in the river!

Slushy green undergrowth
Where the roach swim—
Here we keep our larder,
Cool and full and dim!

Every one for what he likes!
We like to be
Heads down, tails up,
Dabbling free!

High in the blue above
Swift whirl and call—
We are a-dabbling,
Up tails all!

LITTLE TROTTY WAGTAIL

John Clare

Little trotty wagtail,
He went in the rain,
And tittering, tottering sideways
He ne'er got straight again.
He stooped to get a worm,
And looked up to get a fly,
And then he flew away
Ere his feathers they were dry.

Little trotty wagtail,
He waddled in the mud,
And left his little footmarks,
Trample where he would.
He waddled in the water-pudge,
And waggle went his tail,
And chirrupt up his wings
To dry upon the garden rail.

Little trotty wagtail,
You nimble all about,
And in the dimpling water-pudge
You waddle in and out;
Your home is nigh at hand,
And in the warm pigsty,
So little Master Wagtail,
I'll bid you a good-bye.

THE BOY AND THE SHEEP

Ann Taylor

"Lazy sheep, pray tell me why
    In the pleasant field you lie,
Eating grass and daisies white,
    From the morning till the night:
Everything can something do;
    But what kind of use are you?"

"Nay, my little master, nay,
    Do not serve me so, I pray!
Don't you see the wool that grows
    On my back to make your clothes?
Cold, ah, very cold you'd be,
    If you had not wool from me.

"When the farmer comes at last,
    And the merry spring is past,
Cuts my woolly fleece away,
    For your coat in wintry day.
Little master, this is why
    In the pleasant fields I lie."

A BOY'S SONG

James Hogg

Where the pools are bright and deep,
Where the gray trout lies asleep,
Up the river and over the lea,
That's the way for Billy and me.

Where the mowers mow the cleanest,
Where the hay lies thick and greenest,
There to track the homeward bee,
That's the way for Billy and me.

Where the hazel bank is steepest,
Where the shadow lies the deepest,
Where the clustering nuts fall free—
That's the way for Billy and me.

Why little boys should drive away
Little sweet maidens from the play,
Or love to banter and fight so well,
That's the thing I could never tell.

But this I know, I love to play
Through the meadow among the hay;
Up the water and over the lea,
That's the way for Billy and me.

THE HOUSEKEEPER

Charles Lamb

The frugal snail, with forecast of repose,
Carries his house with him where'er he goes;
Peeps out, and if there comes a shower of rain,
Retreats to his small domicile again.
Touch but a tip of him, a horn—'tis well—
He curls up in his sanctuary shell.
He's his own landlord, his own tenant; stay
Long as he will, he dreads no Quarter Day.
Himself he boards and lodges; both invites
And feasts himself; sleeps with himself o'nights.
He spares the upholsterer trouble to procure
Chattels; himself is his own furniture,
And his sole riches. Wheresoe'er he roam,
Knock when you will, he's sure to be home.

ON THE GRASSHOPPER AND THE CRICKET

John Keats

The poetry of the earth is never dead:
    When all the birds are faint with the hot sun,
And hiding in cooling trees, a voice will run
    From hedge to hedge about the new-mown mead;
    That is the Grasshopper's—he takes the lead
        In summer luxury—he has never done
        With his delights; for when tired out with fun,
He rests at ease beneath some pleasant weed.

The poetry of earth is ceasing never;
    On a lone winter evening, when the frost
    Has wrought a silence, from the stove there shrills
The Cricket's song, in warmth increasing ever,
    And seems to one, in drowsiness half lost,
    The Grasshopper's among some grassy hills.

KINDNESS TO ANIMALS

Anonymous

Little children, never give
   Pain to things that feel and live;
Let the gentle robin come
   For the crumbs you save at home—
As his food you throw along
   He'll repay you with a song;
Never hurt the timid hare
   Peeping from her green grass lair,
Let her come and sport and play
   On the lawn at the close of day;
The little lark goes soaring high
   To the bright windows of the sky
Singing as if 'twere always spring,
   And fluttering on an untired wing—
Oh! Let him sing his happy song,
   Nor do these gentle creatures wrong.

LITTLE GIRLS

Laurence Alma Taldema

If no one ever marries me,
    And I don't see why they should,
For nurse says I'm not pretty,
    And I'm seldom very good—

If no one ever marries me,
    I shan't mind very much,
I shall buy a squirrel in a cage,
    And a little rabbit hutch;

I shall have a cottage near a wood,
    And a pony all my own,
And a little lamb, quite clean and tame,
    That I can take to town.

And when I'm getting really old—
    At twenty-eight or nine—
I shall find a little orphan girl
    And bring her up as mine.

SEASONS OF PLAY: THE SUMMER

"Summer is coming, summer is coming,
I know it, I know it, I know it.
Light again, leaf again, life again, love again,"
Yes, my wild little Poet.

Alfred, Lord Tennyson

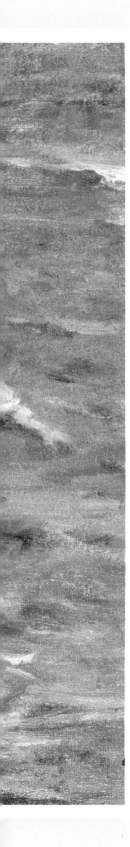

ARIEL'S SONG
William Shakespeare

Come unto these
   yellow sands,
And then take hands:
Curtsied when you
   have, and kiss'd—
The wild waves whist;
Foot it featly here
   and there;
And, sweet sprites,
   the burden bear.
     Hark, hark!
     Bow-wow
The watchdogs bark:
     Bow-wow,
     Hark, hark!
I hear the strain
   of strutting
   chanticleer cry,
Cock-a-diddle-dow.

THE GLADNESS OF NATURE
William Cullen Bryant

Is this a time to be cloudy and sad,
 When our mother Nature laughs around;
When even the deep blue heavens look glad,
 And gladness breathes from the blossoming ground?

There are notes of joy from the hangbird and wren
 And the gossip of swallows all through the sky;
The ground squirrel gaily chirps by his den,
 And the wilding bee hums merrily by.

The clouds are at play in the azure space
 And their shadows at play on the bright green vale,
And here they stretch to the frolic chase,
 And there they roll on the easy gale.

There's a dance of leaves in that aspen bower,
 There's a titter of winds in that beechen tree,
There's a smile on the fruit, and a smile on the flower,
 And a laugh from the brook that runs to the sea.

And look at the broadfaced sun, how he smiles
 On the dewy earth that smiles in his ray,
On the leaping waters and gay young isles;
 Ay, look, and he'll smile thy gloom away.

THE GRASS

Emily Dickinson

The grass so little has to do—
   A sphere of simple green,
With only butterflies to brood
   And bees to entertain,

And stir all day to pretty tunes
   The breezes fetch along,
And hold the sunshine in its lap
   And bow to everything;

And thread the dews all night, like pearls,
   And make itself so fine—
A duchess was too common
   For such a noticing.

And even when it dies, to pass
   In odors so divine,
As lowly spices gone to sleep,
   Or amulets of pine.

And then to dwell in sovereign barns,
   And dream the days away—
The grass has so little to do,
   I wish I were the hay!

LITTLE THINGS

Julia Fletcher Carney

Little drops of water,
  Little grains of sand,
Make the mighty ocean
  And the pleasant land.

So the little moments,
  Humble though they be,
Make the mighty ages
  Of eternity.

So our little errors
  Lead the soul away
From the path of virtue,
  Far in sin to stray.

Little deeds of kindness,
  Little words of love,
Help to make earth happy
  Like the heaven above.

WHAT THE BIRDS SAY
Samuel Taylor Coleridge

Do you ask what the birds say?
The sparrow, the dove,
The linnet and thrush say,
"I love, I love, and I love!"

In the winter they're silent,
The wind is so strong;
What it says I don't know,
But it sings a loud song.

But green leaves and blossoms,
And sunny warm weather,
And singing and loving
All come back together.

But the lark is so brimful
Of gladness and love,
The green fields below him,
The blue sky above,

That he sings, and he sings,
And forever sings he,
"I love my love, and
My love loves me."

THE AUTUMN

The morns are meeker than they were,
The nuts are getting brown;
The berry's cheek is plumper,
The rose is out of town.

The maple wears a gayer scarf;
The field, a scarlet gown.
Lest I should be old-fashioned,
I'll put a trinket on.

Emily Dickinson

AUTUMN FIRES

Robert Louis Stevenson

In the other gardens
   And all up the vale,
From the autumn bonfires
   See the smoke trail!

Pleasant summer over
   And all the summer flowers,
The red fire blazes,
   The gray smoke towers.

Sing a song of seasons!
   Something bright in all!
Flowers in the summer,
   Fires in the fall!

THE KITTEN AND THE FALLING LEAVES

William Wordsworth

See the kitten on the wall,
Sporting with the leaves that fall,
Withered leaves, one, two, and three
From the lofty elder tree,
Through the calm and frosty air
Of the morning bright and fair.

Eddying round and round they sink
Softly, slowly: one might think,
From the motions that are made,
Every little leaf conveyed
Sylph or fairy hither tending—
To this lower world descending

But the kitten, how she starts,
Crouches, stretches, paws, and darts!
First at one, and then its fellow
Just as light and just as yellow;
There are many now—now one—
Now they stop and there are none.

A SONG OF HARVEST HOME

Charles Dickens

Hail to the merry autumn days,
    When yellow cornfields shine
Far brighter than the costly cup
    That holds the monarch's wine.

Hail to the merry harvest time,
    The gayest of the year,
The time of rich and bounteous crops,
    Rejoicing, and good cheer!

A RIDDLE: THE VOWELS

Jonathan Swift

We are little airy creatures,
All of different voice and features;
One of us in glass is set,
One of us you'll find in jet.
T'other you may see in tin,
And the fourth a box within.
If the fifth you should pursue,
It can can never fly away from you.

THE ALPHABET

Kate Greenaway

A was an apple pie;
B bit it;
C cut it;
D dealt it;
E envied it;
F fought for it;
G got it;
H had it;
J jumped for it;
K knelt for it;
L longed for it;
M mourned for it;
N nodded for it;
O opened it;
P peeped in it;
Q quartered it;
R ran for it;
S sang for it;
T took it;
U, V, W, X, Y, and Z
    all had a large slice
    and went off to bed.

ROBIN REDBREAST

William Allingham

Bright yellow, red, and orange, the leaves
    come down in hosts;
The trees are Indian princes, but soon they'll
    turn to ghosts;
The scanty pears and apples hang russet
    on the bough;
It's autumn, autumn, autumn late, 'twill soon
    be winter now.
        Robin, robin redbreast, o robin dear!
            And what will this poor robin do?
              For pinching days are near.

The fireside for the cricket, the wheat stack for
    the mouse,
When gusting night winds whistle and moan
    all 'round the house.
The frosty ways like iron, the branches plumed
    with snow—
Alas! In winter dead and dark, where can poor
    robin go?
        Robin, robin redbreast, o robin dear!
            And a crumb of bread for robin,
              His little heart to cheer.

THE WINTER

Over the land freckled with snow half-thawed
The speculating rooks at their nests cawed
And saw from elm-tops, delicate as flowers of grass,
What we could not see below, winter pass.

Edward Thomas

A SLEDDING SONG

Norman C. Schlichter

Sing a song of winter,
    Of frosty clouds in air!
Sing a song of snowflakes
    Falling everywhere.

Sing a song of winter!
    Sing a song of sleds!
Sing a song of tumbling
    Over heels and heads.

Up and down a hillside
    When the moon is bright,
Sledding is a tiptop
    Wintertime delight.

SNOWFLAKES

Mary Elizabeth Mapes Dodge

Whenever a snowflake leaves the sky,
It turns and turns to say, "Goodbye!
Goodbye, dear cloud, so cool and gray!"
Then lightly travels on its way.

And when a snowflake finds a tree,
"Good day!" it says, "Good day to thee!
Thou art so bare and lonely, dear,
I'll rest and call my comrades here."

But when a snowflake, brave and meek,
Lights on a rosy maiden's cheek,
It starts, "How warm and soft the day!
'Tis summer!" and it melts away.

DIRGE FOR THE YEAR

Percy Bysshe Shelley

As the wild air stirs and sways
    The tree-swung cradle of a child,
So the breath of these rude days
    Rocks the year—be calm and mild,
Trembling hours; Winter will arise
    With new love in her eyes.

THE BELLS
Edgar Allan Poe

Hear the sledges with the bells—
    Silver bells!
What a world of merriment their melody foretells!
    How they tinkle, tinkle, tinkle,
      In the icy air of night!
    While the stars that oversprinkle
    All the heavens seem to twinkle
      With a crystalline delight;
    Keeping time, time, time,
    In a sort of Runic rhyme,
To the tintinnabulation that so musically wells
    From the bells, bells, bells, bells,
      Bells, bells, bells—
From the jingling and the tinkling of the bells.

WINTER
Anonymous

Old Winter is a sturdy one,
    And lasting stuff he's made of;
His flesh is firm as iron-stone,
    There's nothing he's afraid of.

THE CHILDREN'S HOUR
Henry Wadsworth Longfellow

Between the dark and the daylight,
When the night is beginning to lower,
Comes a pause in the day's
    occupations
That is known as the Children's Hour

I hear in the chamber above me
The patter of little feet;
The sound of a door that is opened,
And voices soft and sweet.

A sudden rush from the stairway,
A sudden raid from the hall!
By three doors left ungaurded
They enter my castle wall!

I have you in my fortress,
And will not let you depart,
But put you down into the dungeons
In the round-tower of my heart.

And there I will keep you forever,
Yes, forever and a day,
Till the walls shall crumble to ruin
And molder in dust away.

THE WIND

Robert Louis Stevenson

I saw you toss the kites on high
And blow the birds about the sky;
And all around I heard you pass,
Like ladies' skirts across the grass—
   O wind, a-blowing all day long,
   O wind that sings so loud a song!

I saw the different things you did,
But always you, yourself, you hid.
I felt you push, I heard you call,
I could not see yourself at all—
   O wind, a-blowing all day long,
   O wind that sings so loud a song!

O you that are so strong and cold,
O blower, are you young or old?
Are you a beast of field and tree
Or just a stronger child than me?
   O wind, a-blowing all day long,
   O wind that sings so loud a song!

THE SPRING

The year's at the spring,
And day's at the morn;
Morning's at seven;
The hillside's dew-pearled;

The lark's on the wing;
The snail's on the thorn:
God's in His heaven—
All's right with the world!

Robert Browning

THE DAISIES

Kate Greenaway

You very fine Miss Molly,
 What will the daisies say,
If you carry home so many
 Of their little friends today?

Perhaps you take a sister,
 Perhaps you take a brother,
Or two little daisies who
 Were fond of one another.

SPRING SONG

George Eliot

Spring comes hither,
 Buds the rose;
Roses wither,
 Sweet spring goes.

Soft winds blow,
 Westward born;
Onward go,
 Toward the morn.

FLOWER CHORUS

Ralph Waldo Emerson

O such a commotion under the ground,
    When March called, "Ho, there! Ho!"
Such spreading of rootlets far and wide,
    Such whisperings to and fro!
"Are you ready?" the snowdrop asked,
    "Tis time to start, you know."
"Almost, my dear," the scilla replied,
    "I'll follow as soon as you go."
Then "Ha! Ha! Ha!" a chorus came
    Of laughter sweet and slow,
From millions of flowers under the ground,
    Yes, millions beginning to grow.

SPRING

Thomas Nashe

The fields breathe sweet, the daisies kiss our feet,
Young lovers meet, old wives a-sunning sit;
In every street these tunes our ears do greet:
    Cuckoo, jug-jug, pu-we, to-witta-woo!
    Spring, the sweet Spring!

A SUDDEN SHOWER

James Whitcomb Riley

Barefooted boys scud up the street,
    Or scurry under sheltering sheds;
And schoolgirl faces, pale and sweet,
    Gleam from the shawls about their heads.

Doors bang; and mothers call
    From alien homes; and rusty gates
Are slammed; and high above it all
    The thunder grim reverberates.

And then abrupt—the rain, the rain!
    The earth lies gasping; and the eyes
Behind the streaming windowpanes
    Smile at the trouble of the skies.

The swallow dips beneath the eaves,
    And flirts his plumes and folds his wings;
And under the catawba leaves
    The caterpillar curls and clings.

Within, the baby claps his hands
    And crows with rapture strange and vague;
Without, beneath the rosebush stands
    A dripping rooster on one leg.

SONG: ON MAY MORNING

John Milton

Now comes the bright morning
    star, day's harbinger,
Comes dancing from the east,
    and leads with her
The flowery May, who from her
    green lap throws
The yellow cowslip and the
    pale primrose.
Hail, bounteous May, that dost
    inspire
Mirth and youth and warm
    desire!
Woods and groves are of thy
    dressing,
Hill and dale doth boast thy
    blessing.
Thus we salute thee with our
    early song,
And welcome thee,
    and wish thee long.

First Line Index